Ting!

The Surprising Power of Intuition
to Transform Work & Innovate

ARUPA TESOLIN

Copyright © 2018 Arupa Tesolin

All rights reserved

ISBN:
9780968464588

DEDICATION

To all of you who are searching for purpose and meaning at work

To you who are transforming organizations,

To you who are engaging authenticity, intuition and creativity in the pursuit of innovation

To my daughters Aria & Christina

To Tulshi Sen who taught me to remember more than I've forgotten

ARUPA TESOLIN

CONTENTS

	Acknowledgments	iii
1	Opening Up To Intuition	1
2	Becoming Aware	11
3	A Different Way of Listening	21
4	Intuition Strikes Home	31
5	A Ting Shows Up	38
6	Looking Deeper	53
7	The Energy to Transform	66
8	The Power of Authenticity	78
9	The Heart of Power	93
10	Going Deeper	99
11	Sharing Ting	109
12	Going Beyond	119
	Summary – The 12 Powers of Ting!	123

ACKNOWLEDGMENTS

With thanks to:

Aria Tesolin – Thanks Aria for your invaluable editing wizardry, literary insights, wickedly funny feedback, occasional political cartoons and practical feedback aka "No, he did not say that!" Ting would not be what it is without you.

Brad Kewalramani – Heartfelt thanks to you Brad for helping to emulate the voice of Tony and his business development sensibility, and the hours of great conversations we had in coffee shops last year.

1 OPENING UP TO INTUITION

It was mid-July. A flock of loud squealing seagulls flew past Hermilla's window overlooking the harbor, victorious over their catch of fish. She cast a hopeful glance at the window, with the thought to go outside and get some sun.

Almost simultaneously she heard her computer chime out a 10-minute reminder for her next meeting. She kept her focus. She was writing recommendations for a new Pan-Asian marketing plan.

The light in her office merged with the natural light coming in from the window, signaling the advancing morning. She glanced again at the clock.

Nearly 11:00 a.m, Tony o'clock, she thought, as she prepared to meet him for his first mentoring meeting.

From the opposite end of the building, in the Business Development division, Tony shifted in his chair thinking about his upcoming meeting with Hermila. He'd had advisors before, both male and female. In the past, he had informally sought out successful people to learn how they had became successful. But this time was different. It was the first time he was participating in a more formal process. He wasn't sure what to expect. He wasn't comfortable with uncertainty, which was kind of funny he thought, given that his entire business role was to create certainty by converting prospects into clients.

His manager, Jas, had recommended he try working with a mentor because he thought Tony was ready to take on new roles and challenges. Not that his performance was an issue, as Tony knew, he was always very productive. But within the last 6 months or so, the usual spring in his step was missing. He wasn't getting the kind of attention from his clients that he used to get. Five years and two promotions after graduating from university seemed like a good success record to start with. He was ahead of most of his colleagues in rank and salary.

But what would he say to her? That something was missing and he didn't know what it was? No. That would not fly. He thought he needed something concrete, something related to his work. So, he decided to talk to her about how he could improve opening conversations with his clients and felt optimistic about that. He'd heard good things about Hermilla, that she was focused and creative. He sure didn't want her to think his career direction was anything but upwards.

He bounded up the stairs for the meeting. There, he was struck by the soothing earthy tones in her office and the contrast between her smooth black rock sculptures and the complex cascade of color patterns emanating from the prints hanging on the walls. "Interesting mind", he mused to himself. He knocked on the open door.

"Hermilla?" he enquired. "Hi, I'm Tony from Business Development."

She half turned around to greet him, then smiled as she rose from her chair to face him with a firm and friendly handshake. "Hi, Tony. It's great to meet you. I'm looking forward to getting to know you and working with you. Please sit down. Let's chat a bit." She motioned to a comfortable sitting area in her office and sat down nearby.

Hermilla explained how the formal mentoring

process worked. They would meet weekly or more often, if needed, to talk about whatever they both thought important; they would clarify one or two things that mattered most and focus on these first and it was an open-ended process. What was most important was for Tony to gain both personally and professionally from the experience. "Both are related." she said. "What affects one, affects the other." She also stressed the mentoring process was confidential between the two of them and wouldn't be reflected in feedback to his supervisor or his performance review.

They talked for what seemed like 30 minutes. Hermilla was attentive but Tony did most of the talking - about how it seemed like his clients didn't have time for him like they used to and didn't seem to need or want the kind of advice he was used to giving them. And how he didn't feel like he was connecting with them but following a scripted process that he felt didn't work well.

She asked him about how things were outside of work, and he confided that everything was going very well. He was engaged to his fiancée, Sara, who was amazing, and they were getting married in the fall. His family was well and were very supportive of him.

"That's the hard part," Tony said. "I'm surrounded by all these wonderful people. But I'm zoned.

Something doesn't feel right and I don't know what it is."

Hermilla considered that before she replied. "There's no 'should' in how you feel. It is what it is." She listened while he spoke more and then asked. "Tony, how happy are you at work these days?"

Tony answered "Honestly, not really. I feel like I'm just going through the motions."

"Why do you come then?"

Tony stopped in mid-thinking his next reply. "Huh?"

"It's a real question Tony."

"It's not something I've really thought about. I like the company.

Habit, I guess. I've gotten used to it."

Hermilla looked Tony directly in the eye and asked "What does your intuition say about what's happening?"

"Intuition?" He let out a laugh. "What does intuition have to do with anything? I don't go by my intuition. I've never had anyone here ask me that. I'm trained to identify and seek out clients that are in a situation of pain and share with them how we can fill that gap with our products. Ultimately, I get paid to make revenue targets."

Hermilla interjected. "Well, I can tell you that my intuition tells me that you are neglecting part of who you are and probably limiting yourself."

Tony thought a bit and then responded. "Yes, I may have been limiting myself. But I don't understand how you can pinpoint intuition as the cause. Isn't that a really ambiguous thing?"

"Of course, it is, Tony. As long as it remains unfamiliar to you. But once you are personally clear and open about it, it can get very specific."

"You mean like seeing the future and things like that?" Tony shifted his feet and stared silently.

"Well sometimes," Hermilla continued, "but the truth is closer to being more aware of what's happening day-to-day and being more engaged in what you do, who you are, and what you're communicating. It's about being present."

Tony exhaled slowly, shifted his gaze to the artwork, and then spoke. "I've got to admit, I'm curious about understanding intuition better, but I've never spent much time working with it. I think that I probably don't have an intuitive bone in my body. My role requires me to be so analytically focused. I speak to my clients about their issues and recommend solutions to them to help solve their problems."

"But are you connecting with them?"

"No, not really. It's like I'm conducting a diagnosis, which I'm really good at, and based on what I find I give them a prescription."

"Well, I suggest you spend some time finding out what it's like to be more intuitive when you do that."

"How do I do that?" Tony seemed puzzled.

"Just be attentive - in the moment, in the flow. Notice things that you're not directly thinking about." She continued, "and Tony, one more thing, do you want to be more intuitive?"

"Well, I'm curious to learn more about it. I just don't really know how."

Hermilla reached for her planner as she said "That's okay. By saying 'Yes' to intuition you've taken the first step. That means you're open to having more intuitive experiences. Have a great week and let's talk some more at our next meeting."

Tony looked up at the computer. The clock display was 1:00 pm. "Wow, I can't believe we've been here for two hours. The time really flew by. Thank you so much for your insight. And for being so generous with your time."

"You're really welcome Tony. I think we covered some important ground today. It was worth it."

Ting! Power #1

Say "YES!" to your intuition

2 BECOMING AWARE

Tony was eager to meet with Hermilla for his second mentoring meeting. She had aroused his curiosity about intuition. But he still wasn't sure about what she meant by being more attentive. He thought he was attentive. He had to be to take care of all the minute details of his client contracts. That always required a lot of focus and attention.

One thing he did notice differently was the effect of the wind on his skin. He began to be attentive to how the air around him felt and whether it was windy or still. He seemed to be more aware of his senses. He found the overall effect to be calming.

"Hi, Hermilla," he called from the doorway to her

office.

"Hi, Tony! I'll be with you in just a minute."

Tony stood outside as the V.P. finished her phone call. He noticed that her voice was strong but not stressful, even in the middle of what sounded like a challenging situation with a supplier. He looked again at one of her stone sculptures that looked like a wave. He particularly noticed the contrast of smoothness and dark coolness. He loved that it conveyed both strength and solidity, yet also softness. It was cool to the touch. He had the urge to run his hand over it but resisted.

"Come in Tony," Hermilla called from the office.

"How are you doing today, Hermilla?" he asked, as he extended his hand to her.

"Oh, I'm great but our supplier isn't very receptive. But we'll work it out. We always find a way."

"That's fair. By the way, I really love these sculptures of yours."

"So do I." answered Hermilla, "They're soapstone carvings by an artist I know, who is also a native healer. He spends a lot of time contemplating each piece of rock before he starts carving, making sure he senses their inner forms so he can work with them."

"That's interesting."

"Yes, I think so too. So, how did your week go? What did you learn this week Tony?"

"Well, I began to pay more attention to my intuition, but I don't know how far I've gotten. I'm still uncertain about it. I'm intrigued there's something to be learned this way, although I don't know if it will bring any real results. The how-to part still seems all over the place to me."

"We'll get to meaning and results later. First, let's take a walk."

They went down the elevator and outside the building. Tony could feel a slightly damp cool breeze wafting off the water nearby. It smelled fresh and filled his nostrils with the air of the bay.

They walked a few blocks and came to a shady tree next to a children's playground. An empty picnic table was nearby, so they casually climbed on top and watched what was going on. Several mothers and nannies hovered nearby, watching their preschoolers while they played, chatting lightheartedly.

"Now tell me what you see," Hermilla suggested.

"I love how the kids laughing and playing and running around. They have so much energy. Whoops, one down. But, no. He's up and running towards the slide."

Hermilla stood up and leaned over to touch a nearby tree. "What else do you notice?"

"They're completely spontaneous. They decide and change directions on a whim. They seem to enjoy every moment. And no moment is the same for very long."

Now Tony stood up too and began to balance himself walking along the tops of the railroad ties at the perimeter of the playspace.

"Pure intuitives, wouldn't you say?" Hermilla reflected.

"Yes, I believe so." Tony launched into a short jump into the sand.

"Remember when you were little? What did you especially like to do?"

"Oh, I loved to go swimming. My Dad used to take us to the community pool on the weekends."

"Do you remember how it was when you started

swimming?"

"I do. Initially, I didn't like it. I remember because I was around three years old and other kids were splashing. I didn't like the water on my face. I remember staying near the edge of the shallow end. As soon as I got in up to my waist, I'd run back to the side where it was safe."

Hermilla stepped up carefully, minding her heels, and joined him balancing sideways on the railroad ties. They both faced the playground. "How did you get to enjoy it?"

"Gradually I made friends and we all taught each other. Then I took some swimming lessons. I remember diving off the diving board and swimming in the deep end from the time I was around eight. I loved it."

"What do you think the difference was?" she asked, stepping lightly along the rail.

"I wasn't afraid, for one thing," said Tony, as he jumped into the sand again. "The water was over my head, but I didn't care. It was all about having fun and doing dives and trying things."

"Well that's how we learn best anyway." reflected Hermilla stepping back down into the grass. "By experience."

They began walking back towards the office.

"So, tell me, Tony. Do you think you were any different than those kids running and playing?"

"No. I was just like they are. I don't even remember what happened when we played. Only beginnings and endings, like coming to the park or to my friend's house, and then having to go home."

"So, what happened?"

"Well, I guess I grew up and now I learn differently."

"How many years of school have you had?"

Tony began calculating out loud as they walked. "Let's see…twelve years plus kindergarten, plus five years for my Masters… I'd say about eighteen or so, not counting nursery school and other developmental training."

Hermilla nodded as they stopped to wait for a traffic light. "Don't you think it's taken a lot of time and effort for you to learn to think the way you do?"

"Absolutely. I guess it shouldn't surprise me now that I have to make an effort to be intuitive."

"Not effort, really. It's actually the opposite of effort. Being intuitive is more about undoing your learned perceptions and seeing what's real. That's how it differs from thinking. Thinking requires effort. Don't you find that you get really hungry after a day of thinking?"

"Absolutely, and especially for carbs."

The crossed the street, still talking, while they passed an outdoor cafe. "That's because your brain is working hard and using up a lot of energy when you're working. It needs to replenish the sugars and other chemicals it uses up.

"You'll find after you get used to it, that using your intuition actually gives you more energy. It is a polar shift from the way you're used to thinking about things. It's more about not thinking and letting things, information, ideas, and feelings come to you without effort. If you're used to expending a lot of effort in thinking, like you do in your job, it takes some practice to stop doing that. Have you ever tried to meditate or do yoga?"

He entered the revolving door at the office building after motioning for Hermilla to go first. Then Tony continued "I tried a couple of times, but my thoughts kept going in different directions and I couldn't stay focused."

"Well, that takes time to develop, but it does help unclutter your mind and create space for intuition. Think about it this way. If your mind was a sponge filled with water to capacity, what would you need to do to take in something new?"

"I'd have to squeeze something out to make room. That's a good analogy."

"Yes, it is. Thinking the way we've been taught has become a habit. Most people aren't aware that it's become a cognitive preference because it's a popular thinking style for our time. They're not as aware they have a choice, and the options include having a more intuitive thinking style, or rather a non-thinking style, if you get what I mean."

They both stopped to wait for the elevator. "Sure, I do, but how do you overcome all that conditioning?"

"Where there's a will, there's a way. My advice is to start by doing nothing for 5 minutes a day. Absolutely nothing. Just be aware of your thoughts, senses, feelings and what's going on within you. This is not really meditation, but it's a prelude to being more self-aware. It's like squeezing the water from the sponge. This short practice will help you recover a sense of presence within yourself. If you're outwardly focused most of the day, you need to do this just for self-preservation. Let me know how it works for you."

They quietly walked back to their respective offices. Tony was busy, doing nothing.

Ting! Power #2

Do nothing for 5 minutes every day

3 A DIFFERENT WAY OF LISTENING

It was raining the next time Tony ran up the stairs to meet Hermila in her office. He noticed the soft sounds the drops made on the windows. They soothed him. He was looking forward to today. These authentic conversations marked the beginning of a new adventure. Although he couldn't see it coming together yet, he felt he was on the right track.

As they sat down together Hermilla asked him to talk about some of the things he wanted to focus on in his career. He spoke about how clients who used to take up a lot of his time weren't calling as much, and when he called them, they weren't really communicating. Despite this, he continued to persist and maintain a friendly rapport with them. He just didn't feel he was getting anywhere.

Hermila asked him about the other Account Managers and what their sales results were. Tony replied that they were down slightly overall, but that his performance was consistent. "What does your intuition say about this?" he asked inquisitively. "I'd really like to know because frankly I just don't see the connection here."

"Hmmm," she said. "They aren't always easy to see. But let's consider how intuition used to happen in early mankind."

"Well," Tony remarked, "from what I understand, it was a kind of visceral instinctive sense that warned them of danger or predators in their environment."

"That's right," affirmed Hermila. "What happened when they got it wrong?"

"I guess they either got good at it or they died. The threats were severe enough that they didn't get many second chances."

"Yes, I think that's true. The gene pool didn't carry their errors too far. But things are a lot different now. Most of the dangers we face, aside from an abrupt accident or something that's mortally obvious, don't harm us right away. Instead, they work bit by bit, over time, by turning up the stress level gradually or incrementally until we reach some critical point like heart disease or other illness.

"Similarly, if we make mistakes in life through improper handling of money or relationships, they don't all break down at once, but over time. Then one day we find ourselves buried in debt or suffering a relationship breakdown. In the workplace or in business, the same thing happens.

"If we make small mistakes, they may go unnoticed. But over time they add up to a performance breach in the form of a self-limiting career, a job loss, the loss of an important client or contract. Possibly, when many people are involved, this can mean the death of a whole organization or part of it."

"So," Tony interjected, "are you saying that being more intuitive helps us anticipate these small changes so we can make decisions to go forward in better ways?"

"Yes, absolutely. How many projects have you seen go bad, because they were already bad in the early stages, and not deeply thought through enough."

"Many," he replied.

"What did you learn from these experiences?"

Tony laughed. "Mostly to avoid getting involved in another one or not taking the risk of working with that same project manager again."

"So, how did it contribute to the whole organization or team and what they learned from it?"

"It had a negative impact," Tony answered.

"Right. And when we do nothing about that, the overall impact gets repeated many times. Each time the organization fails in a small way, it impacts the individual motivations of everyone involved in it. It's a descending spiral that starts off slowly and ambiguously.

"Let me tell you what I learned from a walnut tree one summer. It was many years ago now, but at the time I was 8 months pregnant with my son Daniel. The doctor had ordered me off work with complete bed rest because I was retaining fluid and there was a medical risk. I absolutely hated it, keeping still and not being able to do things, like I was used to. I thought of all the things I wanted to do before the baby came. But I couldn't or the next step would be a hospital bed.

"So, I sat in the backyard on a lounge chair under our walnut tree. Now this tree had always been there, but I hadn't really noticed it much. When I began to see it day after day, I'd notice things. I knew it was a very fast growing tree because it had so many little branches that continually died, and many new branches that continually grew to compensate for it.

"I began to realize that because the new growth was always so green and healthy, it didn't matter how old the tree was. It was always young where the new branches grew. This became an analogy for me about life and organizations. You always have to look for the new growth. Intuition definitely has a role in helping us find it and reminding us of where to look."

She continued. "These days, we all want quick answers and simple solutions. As the world grows more complex, our intellect struggles to try to find them, but can't, because it's too slow. Meanwhile, all the media, images and ideas we're exposed to tend to starve off our quieter intuitive knowing. We get stressed trying to figure it all out.

"Early man relied on a primitive kind of brain, also called the amphibious or reptilian brain. But this 'turtle brain" can't handle complexity, because the control center for finding intuitive solutions has migrated further up our brain stem, where higher intelligence, reasoning and learning skills reside. On top of this having all that stress muddies up the signals."

Tony interjected. "So, we need to use our intuition so we can be more perceptive about the early warning signs of a wrong direction or approach?"

"Yes, logic, analysis, and all our streamlined operational processes rarely give us this information early enough. Intuition does, but we all need to become better listeners to the ways intuition speaks to us."

"Then maybe I need to be more perceptive about listening to my clients" concluded Tony, "and find new ways to engage them or come up with other things they might need. I might have to change a few things to do it."

"So long as you're not undermining our values and making an honest effort to learn, I don't think you're going to compromise anything. You might end up teaching us all something new."

"Okay, I'm on board. By the way, I've been doing that exercise you suggested about doing nothing for five minutes a day."

"How's it working out?"

"Well, the first few days were really hard. It sounded like such a short amount of time, but I just couldn't keep still for that long. Now, I'm beginning to get relaxed and I kind of enjoy it. I notice more things - sounds, senses, things going on around me. Funny how I just didn't notice them before. Now they're a source of joy in my day."

"That's good," said Hermilla. "Now, try extending it to 10 minutes a day. Just focus on your breathing and what's going on internally. Let thoughts come and go without being attached to them, like watching waves on the ocean. If you find yourself getting distracted, gently bring yourself back to your breathing. This is a way to build your awareness.

"You've been educated to become a thinker, so you need to prepare yourself to be more intuitive before it's needed. Intuition is like high-speed internet. It's always on. But it would be too much too fast to go straight to this. So, it's more like getting started on 'dial-up', if you can even remember those days," she said with a smile, "before moving to a higher speed bandwidth. It's a little slower, but it works. Good luck with your clients this week."

"Thanks, Hermilla. And thanks so much for taking the time to share your insights with me and opening me to a part of myself that I really didn't know was there. I'm beginning to appreciate the benefits of being more perceptive."

"It works both ways, Tony. I too enjoy contributing in some way to your growth. I'm always looking for new mentors for myself too.

"Even that tree was my mentor for a while."

Ting! Power #3

Practice awareness for 10 minutes every day

4 INTUITION STRIKES HOME

The sun was barely up when Tony emerged outdoors for an early morning jog. The smell of leaves caressed the damp air. It was early fall and a bit of yellow was visible in the trees. Everything else was still green.

He listened consciously to the plompfh, plompfh, plompfh of his running shoes as they met the pavement. It was quiet and still. Morning activities and the sound of traffic building on the highway were far away from the little chirping noises of the chipmunks and squirrels as they popped in and out of the trees in the park.

So nice to get in an early morning run. Tony mused,

as a sudden urge to visit his mother nearby popped into his mind. He figured he'd run the next few blocks and join her for breakfast today. She was usually up by this time.

He arrived in the driveway and aimed for the side door, chiming "Hellooo! It's me."

"Hi, son!" Marianna's melodious and loving voice found his ear before her image did. Then she came around the corner with a warm hug and kiss. "You must have been up early today. Got time for a coffee?"

"Yes, that's why I came by. Thought it would be nice to spend a few minutes with you before work. Where's Dad, fishing?"

"Yes. He left early to go down to the lake. You know how much he loves to fish this time of year because it's still warm. He's got a mind to catch a nice big salmon. He caught a small one last week."

She looked at her perspiring son, dark-haired curls falling into his eyes and his slightly lop-sided smile that still reminded her of her younger boy. She loved the man he'd become - so intelligent and caring. She couldn't wait to see her grandchildren that would arrive in future years. Turning back to the stove, she reached over to grasp the coffee cup, and suddenly went limp.

Meanwhile, in no time Tony had flown across the room and caught her just before she hit the floor. It was a soft landing, cushioned by her son. He cradled her head in his arms. "Ma! Ma! What's wrong? What happened?"

She lay there groggy, not sure of what happened. She heard his voice calling her and weakly responded. "I... don't know... what happened."

He sat her up. "You fainted! Are you okay?"

"Just dizzy a bit, Tony....help me up."

He lifted her up and helped her to sit down on the kitchen chair.

"You okay now?"

"Getting better," she replied, a little more strongly. "You sure picked a good time to be here."

"No kidding. You could've been really hurt if the fall was harder! Is everything okay with you? Has anything like this ever happened before?"

"Never Tony, but I've been getting a few dizzy spells once in a while. Thought it was because I was just getting older."

"Well, we'd better take you to the doctor and get everything checked out."

"Yes, you're right. I'll call and ask your father to take me as soon as he gets back. He'll be here anytime."

A few minutes later his car pulled into the driveway and they all discussed what happened. They decided they would see the doctor that day if they could and told Tony he should get going to work. Marianna assured him that she would call later to let him know the results.

Tony went on to work, disturbed in thought, wondering again what would have happened if he had not been there.

He called Hermilla and asked if they could meet a few minutes earlier to talk to her about something personal that had happened. She agreed. He went up to her office and explained what had happened with his mother that morning.

Clearly, he'd had an intuitive call to action to go there. The thought had unexpectedly come up and he followed through. It was the easiest thing to do. "Why" he wondered aloud, "did this idea just show up all of a sudden?"

Hermilla looked at him with both concern and care. "We can't understand everything, Tony; why things happen to the ones we love. But we have to trust that when it's important for us to know something, we usually get to know. That is if we aren't too stressed and distracted to be attentive to these sudden thoughts. That's the way our intuition communicates."

He described to her how he had been set instantly in motion, moving towards his mother even before she faltered. It was a natural, timeless response. It happened as if it had been choreographed.

Hermilla continued. "From what I know, intuition is more immediate when imminent danger or harm is involved. It seems to be more evident in these kinds of circumstances than in your work where you're thinking about sales targets, client needs, and all the technical details you're preoccupied with."

And then, with care, she added "I hope your mom will be okay. Please let me know how she makes out."

"I will," replied Tony. "Hermilla, thanks for being there for me to talk about this. It was confusing for me to understand what had happened today. I deeply appreciate that you've helped me understand the importance of intuition and helping me to open up to it. These exercises I've been doing have made me more attentive. Today of all days, it helped me in a totally unexpected way to be at the right place at the right time without having to try."

"You bet it did, Tony. Even with my son and daughter, I listen to them in two ways - what they say to me and what I sense intuitively. If both don't match, there's something more I need to know. So, I make sure that, as busy as I am, I take the time to be clear and to listen. It's important for me and for them. Of course, that doesn't stop there. I bring it into my work. I can't tell you how many times I've pinpointed a problem on a deal or project, where there was no other way I could have known about it otherwise because the indicators were never there. It's just like 'Ting!' a little warning bell goes off and insight comes. Then I dig into it further and find something that was really important to know about."

He looked at her. "Ting? I like that word."

"Just keep listening, Tony, not just with your ears, but with your whole self."

"Yes, I'll do that Hermilla. See you later."

Ting! Power #4

Listen to your intuition.
Notice your Ting's

5 A TING! SHOWS UP

New project plans. Clients on the line. Problems to fix. Tony's mind was racing. What to do first? He was not so subtly aware of the timeline for the monthly revenue report looming ahead of him, with little to project in new revenues so far. In fact, they were shrinking. He hadn't been able to close any new deals yet. He decided to reschedule two meetings and call back his priority clients, especially the ones he'd not heard from in the past month.

His line rang again. He picked it up on the first ring. It was Sheryl, the Operations VP for one of his major clients. "Tony," she said, "we have to cancel the implementation of our development project with you."

He talked with her a bit and found out that her company was stream-lining several divisions to cut costs. One of the cuts was their project with his company, which had been in the final budget approval phase. True to his professional ability, Tony carefully documented the reasons and tried to find a way, any way, to make the project work.

He suggested scaling it down, postponing it instead of canceling, redeveloping the timelines and scope, changing the payment structure - in short, everything he could think of. In the end, there was nothing, nothing they were open to. He ended the call on a note of optimism that things would improve before long, said good-bye and hung up. But a mood of pensiveness hung on him silently and would not let go.

Soon another call came in. This time it was a scale-down of a project that was in the end phase, resulting in a modified purchase agreement at a reduced cost. His mood continued nagging at him. A few more calls followed to resolve issues with other departments and clients. It was almost noon already. And still, Sheryl was in his mind.

Finally, he stopped. "What is this?" he said to himself. Behind all the racing and pace of the day, there was a deep hole. He felt it, fathomed it, swam in it, but with his deeper perception, not with his thoughts and intellect. "There's something more here, something I'm missing," he knew intuitively, "I'm going to find out what it is."

He called Sheryl back. She was having lunch at her desk. "Hi Sheryl, it's me Tony again. Do you mind if we chat for a bit?"

"Not at all," she said.

"Sheryl," he asked "is everything okay between us? Is there anything you think I could be doing better for you as a client?"

"Tony," she answered, "We've been working together for a long time. You know that's not what it is or I would have told you straight up. We've always partnered well together and I do enjoy working with you."

"Thanks for that. I just feel like there's something else I might be missing. What else is happening there, Sheryl? Would you mind filling me in a little, if you can?"

They talked for a long time. Tony listened without responding, without thinking, and without trying to have an action plan in the back of his mind. It was business as unusual. He heard about the quality problems they were having across their international divisions that resulted in the use of a lot of scarce resources. The need to track, re-track and correct so many different things with different standards was a statistical and resource nightmare. The more they talked, the more he began to feel that this was all way way over his head.

He felt the sense of overwhelm. But he chose to not respond to that. Instead, he continued to listen. When they were finished, he explained that he could understand why they wanted to cancel the project. There was simply no resource complement available for them to do it and carry on business at the same time. He resolved to continue to be there for her and her company in whatever way he could whenever they were ready to move forward. And he let go of the need to solve their problem.

He moved on. It was a full day. His own company was in the middle of implementing a new customer relationship management system. CRM was the acronym everyone was using. Some of the more experienced account managers were having difficulty accepting the new activities and were questioning its value. They thought it machined the process and got in the way of the natural conversations they were used to having with their customers. The younger staff, who had grown up with technology, adapted to it right away and didn't really ask questions like that.

But he thought they were good questions. Tony wondered about the connection between CRM and intuitive relationships. He thought about ways to use it for onboarding with new clients, not just responding to customer preferences, but creating an opportunity to ask open questions about their experience and why they thought the way they did. He felt sure that there were ways it could be used to get insights that people hadn't even thought of.

It was an active day. Things happened. And more things happened. He was still in his office at 7:00 p.m. and then he left.

That night he had a dream. He watched as birds lined up on a suspended wire and flew away really fast. Then new birds came to fill all the spots. Suddenly the birds changed direction and reversed. They flew away and then lined up. More dreams followed, but when he awoke in the morning, he only remembered the birds and wondered what the dream meant.

Another busy day followed. He met with his manager, Jas, who asked how his mentoring program was going. With so many other issues going on, they hadn't had time to talk about it.

"It's going really well, I think, Jas. And it isn't at all what I expected."

"Oh," said Jas, mildly curious, "How so?"

"Well, believe it or not, I'm learning a lot about my intuition."

"Intuition is a very powerful thing," replied Jas. He then told Tony about a school colleague who went on to start up a company because he'd had an intuition while riding his motorcycle to work in India.

"That's interesting" answered Tony. There's an obvious connection between insight and invention. Nikola Tesla is a great example of that. It's like he had the keys to the universe with his supercharged intelligence, and engineering was his way of expressing it."

"That's so true" Jas added. "Actually, Tesla foresaw the internet, wireless communication, and free electricity throughout the world, even in the early 1900's. He had a relentless mind and a passionate commitment to his visions."

"What was really interesting is the way he visualized. In his moment of insight, he'd see full working electrical and mechanical schematics. He had this intuitive sensibility that, once he saw them, he "knew" they would work. His sense of conviction about that was astonishing.

"He had a relationship with universal intelligence that made electrical and mechanical engineering look like poetry."

Tony added, "Yes, his stature was clearly underrated during his time. Only later, after realizing how enormous his contributions were, do we really appreciate his genius. He was a verifiable genius -- the Steve Jobs of his era."

"I would agree with that." said Jas "The power of intuition is in how it gives us a way to elucidate the unknown. When people are able to accurately tap into that, they can do much more than they thought they could. Intuition gives you a line of sight that's not limited by your thoughts or beliefs. "

They ended up talking about the different ways people perceive intuition - how some people have visions, others experience a positive feeling to do something, some people feel bodily sensations in their gut or heart, and others suddenly just know. They talked about how intuition communicates in dreams and happens at the times we're most relaxed, like in the shower or when the body is physically occupied and thoughts are clear, like during a run.

They agreed it was important to pay attention to them and to the meaning and metaphors underneath the thoughts. Often just a hint can lead to an insight.

Tony left the meeting feeling somewhat surprised at how receptive Jas was to the idea of him using more intuition in his work.

In the middle of a second coffee, Tony suddenly received a 'Ting!'

"Whoa, what was that?" he said aloud.

He suddenly saw, in the form of a vision, the image of a working system that resolved many divergent production issues. He remembered the birds he saw in his dream and how they began reversing the way they lined up.

He immediately thought of Sheryl's company and the problems they were having.

"Could this be a way to fix them?" he wondered.

One of the key things he was seeing was a reversal of existing processes and reporting systems. But this kind of integrated resourcing and consulting solution was way beyond his scope in sales. He arranged quickly to go and discuss his idea with Jas that afternoon as a potential solution to present to Sheryl's company.

When they did meet, Tony outlined his concerns

about the context, and Jas agreed that it was outside his department's scope. But a research division in another city had taken on projects of that nature from time to time. Jas said he'd get in touch with them to see if a project could be done and within the time scope time they needed.

It was nearly the end of the day before Jas hurriedly breezed through Tony's office and gave him the green light and some details. "Call your client and see if they'd be interested," he said.

Tony called Sheryl. She wasn't in. Time ticked. He didn't know whether she'd left for the day. At five minutes before six, his phone rang. It was Sheryl calling him back. He explained what they had come up with. He said it would involve another division and they felt confident they could have the company back on track within 90 days. They proposed to develop a customized resource system that would replace the other project. She listened and felt the project might really get wings.

There were those birds again. Tony confided the solution had come to him partly in a dream.

Sheryl laughed. "I believe in that," she said. "Now if only we could get that kind of insight when we wanted to. It just sort of happens." Then, she asked him for a detailed proposal that she could present to their executive committee.

The next few days were a blur. The proposal was prepared and Tony returned to other business.

The evenings were more peaceful as he spent time with Sara and their friends. She had discovered a book of romantic poetry and, partly as a joke, asked Tony if he would like to read them with her. He did, and they both started laughing. It turned out to be so much fun and so fulfilling that they decided to read a new one together every night.

He also kept in close contact with his Mom and Dad. She was still running through tests at the hospital but did not have any more episodes since that day. He, strangely, was not worried about the results. In fact, he welcomed them.

Tony also deepened his time with the breathing exercises late at night, which turned into a real calming zone for him. He felt alive, light and peacefully alert.

During the day, his energy level returned. He was certainly busy with a full life of work, plus wedding planning, but things seemed to be in a flow and he felt he was no longer running to catch up. The flow was everywhere and he was at its center, everywhere present.

On Tuesday morning Sheryl called back with happy news. The new project had been unanimously approved. It was going to be a big challenge and there were some major sticking points, but nonetheless, it was a go, partly based on the trust they had built with Tony and his company over the years.

"Your associates are certainly going to be busy," she said. And Tony knew she was right.

By the time Thursday arrived, it seemed that the world had changed since he last saw Hermilla.

"Hermilla," he said, "I finally got a sense of what that a Ting is. You'll never believe how it happened." He explained everything to her, the declining business reports, his activities with clients, his discussions with Sheryl, his dream, the project… everything.

She listened to everything, saying nothing, only observing and being attentive.

He stopped. And silence filled the spaces of her office.

It was a long silence; a good silence.

Finally, Hermilla spoke, "My grandmother and

grandfather were farmers. They owned a lot of land and raised both vegetables and livestock. They were doing quite well for their time and weren't in need of anything. Then a civil war broke out in their territory and, for a while, it seemed that they were going to survive its difficulties.

But then one night my grandfather had a dream and he woke up my grandmother and said, "We're leaving now. Go get the children…" there were 4 of them, "on the carriage and take our savings, I'll get the horses." At 4:30 in the morning they quietly left the village destined for no place in particular. They traveled to different villages for almost two months until they found a new place, bought a little plot of land and built, over time, a new home. It was tough. They found out later that, within a few hours on the same day they left, a group of mercenary bandits had massacred everyone in the village and burned down all the homes. So, in the end, I exist today because of his intuition."

Tony nodded, understanding.

"Dreams," she said "are a good way of communicating directly to us something that would take too long for us to figure out. When it's time to change something, that's when a 'Ting' arrives if we are willing to see it."

"Tony, do you know the meaning of clairvoyance?"

"Doesn't that mean an ability to see the paranormal?"

"It means to see clearly. Clairvoyance means to see what is."

They talked more about Tony's work and interim goals - both personal and professional. As time moved on, the day's remaining tasks swallowed them both.

Ting! Power #5

Pay attention to your Ting's. Look deeper.

Tingi lower is

an invitation to your feelings.
Look deeper.

6 LOOKING DEEPER

The next few weeks flew by quickly. Tony was almost too busy to pay attention as he juggled his time among his regular clients, working on the new project with Sheryl, and discussing the project with new colleagues in the Research group.

He was used to a certain level of progress and predictable developments. The Research people operated differently. Ruggedly creative; their approaches were often experimental. They liked to 'color outside the lines.'

They spent more time talking and planning, rather than developing, at the beginning of any project and were multi-disciplinary. Technical specialists worked alongside marketing and creative people, product development, and communications. They invested more time at off-site meetings at the clients' business, looking at what different people did, poking into process gaps and bottlenecks and evaluating the inter-relationships with other departments, asking questions, and making suggestions.

Tony was aware that this wider net of variables brought with it an almost bewildering context and exposed multiple seas of changing expectations. But he found this invigorating and challenging and thought his new team members were interesting. Gradually the scope narrowed and the project began to take shape and move ahead.

Every day they developed a new list of take-forward initiatives. This required Tony to cross-reference, do research, and propose solutions. He began talking with Sheryl several times a day. One day, after a strenuous discussion, they began to chat lightheartedly. It was something they both needed – a break.

"Wouldn't it be easier," Tony proposed, "if we just could do this intuitively?"

"For sure," Sheryl laughed. "If we had approached the whole process more intuitively, in the beginning, we'd have been better able to anticipate the need for these developments earlier. But you know, that's the world we live in. You might get an intuitive idea, but it still takes a world of logicians, technologists and people masters to implement it."

"Yes, maybe that's the reason I wasn't able to comprehend your real needs earlier. You needed a solution we weren't offering you. These things can be so hard to figure out."

"Well Tony, a product doesn't ask its mother "What's going to happen to me after I die?""

"Quite true." replied Tony. "That's not something we as product makers tend to ask either. That's a mind-blowing observation. We definitely should be asking that question. The answer would probably lead us to new solutions."

"I think you're right," Sheryl paused, "If we asked questions like this and spent time honing our intuitive smarts, many things could be simpler and easier, even human relations. Ninety percent of the barriers I see, if they're not process and quality related, they are about how people interpret and communicate."

"I wonder," Tony said aloud, "What do you think this actually cost a business?"

"I'll bet it affects at least a third of our output,"

Sheryl answered without hesitation. "In business overall, this probably costs companies millions, maybe even billions, not to mention what we might be losing out on in innovation, new products and services, or reducing our time-to-market cycles. Or even providing a meaningful experience for people who work here.

"When you take time to really think about and evaluate it, the economic and human losses that result from our lack of - let's call it our 'intuitive agility – are staggering. What a waste of time and energy!"

"Our largest business problem right now is staff disengagement. It's become an epidemic. People just aren't present. And we respond to that by putting together a massive set of procedures that we expect them to carry out with robotic precision. But their creativity, intuition and personal aspirations don't get affirmed, so they tune out. That's how we lose them."

"I can relate to that," said Tony. "I've seen it here too. What do you think the solution is?"

"Take it seriously. Talk about it. Give people more flexibility and span of control. More range with less restriction."

"But then you'd have to trust them to carry it out in

good faith."

"You bet. When you look at most corporate expectations today, they're set up to audit failure, not success. That's a big disincentive for people. It continues right up to the CEO level. He or she has a set of almost unmanageable contingencies, and their decisions are often limited by their boards, who want to micromanage everything. That's why it's more fashionable to fire the CEO instead of changing the internal culture that creates these conditions."

"That's true, Sheryl, it all leads to a severe case of inner gridlock that constrains thinking and creativity. I know we can talk further about this. If you have any ideas about other ways we can improve things for you, please tell me."

"Well, I wonder what we could do to encourage intuition as a way of opening the door to more creative contribution by our staff," Sheryl mused.

"I've been wondering the same. Maybe start a few conversations about it and see how receptive people are. Or have some lunch & learn events." Tony suggested. "If you start talking about it, others will too. I'm thinking about how to do something like that here.

"Recently I got involved in a mentoring process that's really opened me up to new possibilities with intuition. In fact, your project was a direct result of it. I've become more curious, not only about my own potential, but about others too. I haven't had a chance to talk about it internally yet. Give me some time to do that and we can pick up this conversation later this week. Maybe we can collaborate a bit."

"Sounds good. Let me give it some thought."

That afternoon Tony met with Jas and they talked about the subject of intuition again. Not surprisingly, based on their earlier conversation, Tony found him very receptive.

"Tony" Jas said, "all humans need to grow and for that they need food. But that food is not only physical. We also need to feed the emotional and spiritual aspects of our being. We haven't done a good job of nurturing whole intelligence in organizations. It's time we fed those other hungers, in ways that align with our business vision."

"I have challenges with the business vision part aligning with whole intelligence," said Tony. "I mean, we seem to put numeric values ahead of everything else. Our business has always been numbers driven. More sales, more profits. That's it."

"If that's it, Tony, we need to do a better job of

communicating why we're in the game. There's more to it than that."

"Try me," Tony suggested playfully.

"Why do you think we're in business, Tony?"

"To make money, obviously," Tony answered.

"Anything else?"

Tony reflected briefly, then said "To be the best at what we do. We try hard at that."

"Yes, that's right," Jas added. "That's how we add value. But the end game is greatness. The real reason we are in business and can stay in business is that we are contributing to progress for the greater good of humanity. This is where value begins. Revenue and profit is one of the ways we measure this."

"I never thought of it that way," Tony replied.

"Let me give you a little more context," said Jas. "All businesses start originally as an insight or idea that inspired an entrepreneur to take action.

"The word 'entrepreneur,' comes from two words – 'entre,' which means 'between' and 'pren', which comes from the French verb 'entreprendre' and means 'to undertake', or in colloquial terms 'to take on.' So, at a certain point that one person's idea becomes bigger than just them.

"So next, we have the job of enlisting others to take it on and help create that vision. We have to get them to see its potential and get excited about making it happen. At that point, it becomes, in today's terms, a start-up.

"Numerics and profit are the easiest things to measure for any business. So, maybe it means that businesses who only measure this are essentially lazy," Jas said with a smile. "But more to the point, the other aspects are fuzzy and harder to quantify. And we lack the tools to do it easily.

"The truth is, we need to start finding ways to amplify and measure purpose. This isn't easy to quantify either. Purpose is best expressed by telling a story. Our goal should be to make business as relevant as movies and literature in the telling of human stories and achievement.

"For the most part organizations, once they reach a certain point of success and begin to optimize that success, become institutions of thinking. They start with dreamers, then the lean managers and bean counters take over.

"The prevailing theory around people and motivation is that we can't tell them what to think, but we can tell them how to behave. But the fact is those behaviors do steer their thinking to certain ends. Then we get stuck because that isn't natural. It's deceptive and manipulative.

"So instead, we have to tell people what we are really about, what we think and feel and want to create and communicate how and who that helps. Then we can attract people who are moved by that. Then it's not a false purpose for them because they already believe in it. When the right talent is attracted to a vision, the actions they take in their work are naturally motivated. They become more fulfilled by being with us."

"It sounds like," Tony offered, "we need to create the cultural affinity to attract the right people."

"Exactly so, Tony." Jas agreed. "For purpose to take hold, we need to get better at being a 'feeling' organization. We need to enable people to be themselves. And get better as an organization at feeling and thinking together. Then more innovation will happen. Transformation is key.

"Human creativity and inspiration are at the top of every personal development scale. The success of any organization relates directly to how well people appreciate one another and how well people are encouraged to contribute their best.

"Intuition also relates to innovation because it's a creative linkage for inventiveness. Once you identify the linkages, it's easy."

"The thing is, you can produce a widget without caring, but when you do care, its value goes up immensely."

"Jas," replied Tony, "This is such a refreshing and very interesting conversation. I appreciate that we are having it. I've never heard this expressed this way before. And I agree with you about connecting the invisible dots. I really like that approach. I'm kind of surprised we've never talked about it earlier. How do you think we can share these ideas further in our organization?"

Jas suggested "Have you thought of maybe starting a short newsletter or an internal podcast? It will get these deeper conversations going. You can ask people for ideas, good stories and examples."

"I like that idea," replied Tony. "We can test it first and see how people respond."

"Yes," said Jas. "If the response is good, we'll take the next step. If not, we'll go back to the drawing board and connect some more dots. I'll help you. What do you think?"

"Sounds good," answered Tony.

"You never know until you try something, right? Tony, you can count on me. I'm very keen about this too. We have a responsibility to unleash motivation and we haven't done enough to nurture it yet."

"Sounds like it might provoke interest if we do it right," Tony interjected.

"Yes," smiled Jas. "The possibilities are infinite. As my familiar teacher Bhinder Done Dat once said, "You can't keep learning from yesterday if you don't learn from today." Tony left his office laughing.

Ting! Power #6

Connect the dots.
Look for opportunities.

7 THE ENERGY TO TRANSFORM

It had rained in the night. The path was damp with leaves, the air a bit chilly. Tony was almost finished his run when he made a last-minute decision to stop by his parents' house after glancing at his watch, imagining they would both be sitting at breakfast.

In fact, they were, with a fresh cup of coffee waiting for him. "We had a feeling you'd come by," said his father, "We just finished talking about it five minutes ago."

"I must've gotten your message," Tony said. "I guess you Tinged me."

"Tinged?" asked his mother.

"Yes, that's the word I use to describe when I get an intuition," answered Tony. "I just had a vision of you and Dad having breakfast, so I decided to come by."

He explained that he was paying more attention to his intuition and had started to meditate. This was helping him to be more intuitive. "You know, a year ago I might have had a similar experience, but I would've completely ignored it. Probably because I was not paying attention back then. My mind was always racing about things that I had to get done. Now, I've learned to be more aware and in the present. I'm way less tense. When I think back to the way I used to be, I can really see how stressed I was. Now that I can get quiet with myself, I see a big difference."

"Tell me more about Ting! they both asked. "What kind of intuition are you talking about?"

"All kinds," said Tony. "Sometimes, like today, it's a sudden urge to see someone or call. Other times, I get a mental flash or an idea that comes along with an energy, urging me to move in a certain direction. Sometimes, I suddenly remember a dream I had while I'm doing something, and it gives me an insight. Sometimes it's a gut feeling; like 'this feels good' or 'this feels bad', kind of thing. It's always different. And that's not the end. I've found that the

Ting! is really the beginning.

"So, what it means for me is, when it happens, I've learned to pay attention and look deeper. A couple weeks ago, I had this dream about birds coming and going. I didn't understand what it meant. The next day I suddenly remembered it while talking with one of my clients. I got the feeling that something was possible but wasn't happening. So, I paid attention to that. Later on, that dream gave me an idea about a possible fix to a big problem they had, which could have been an even bigger problem for my company if I didn't find a solution, because the client is a big account."

"Well, you do seem a lot more relaxed lately, even though I know you've been working a lot of hours," said his father.

"This has done you some good. And hey, if it brings you out here for breakfast more often, it works for me!" He smiled.

"Speaking of breakfast," his mother intervened, "do you know that your Dad has been getting up to go fishing earlier so he can come back and make me breakfast in the morning? He's made breakfast every day for two weeks now. He's even starting to go grocery shopping to look for different vegetables and things to cook."

"Tony, you know I take care of my sweetheart. She's my number one. I know you'd do the same for Sara."

Tony smiled, thinking of Sara. He knew his father was right.

Martino continued. "It's a good thing we found out your mother's health is going to be okay with a few lifestyle changes. That low blood sugar episode hasn't happened again so far and we're going to make sure it doesn't."

"Yes," Tony agreed, looking affectionately at both of them, "I had a feeling that it wasn't anything too serious."

"Another Ting!?" his mother asked.

"I think so," grinned Tony. "Something inside told me it was going to be okay and not to worry."

"You know," Tony said, "These Ting!'s are really helpful. In fact, I'm going to do a newsletter at work to help people talk more openly and share their experience with intuition. I don't have a name for it yet."

"Well why not call it Ting!?" said Martino.

"Ting!? Sure. That would be a good name. Then I can explain what a Ting! is. It would be a good conversation starter."

Tony checked his watch. "Oh, it's getting late. I'd better go. Catch you later."

They walked him to the curb and watched as he began his run home. He didn't see them smiling at him and at each other in his wake, but he could feel it.

Later that day, he met with Hermilla and updated her on what was happening and with his new project. She was impressed. They began to review the reasons for starting the mentoring process.

"So, how's your energy level now?" Hermilla asked.

"Really great," answered Tony. "I've gone from wondering whether I'm in the right place doing the right thing to being in the right place doing the right thing. When I look back, I can't believe the way I was before. I feel so alive, like everything is happening before my eyes. I look forward to coming to work again and I look forward to leaving at the end of the day too. But now I feel like I'm accomplishing something. I have a reason to be here and I've got something meaningful to contribute."

"Great!" responded Hermilla. "How about your professional development? You and Jas thought it would be good for you to extend your experience into new areas."

"That is exactly what's happening with my new project. It's taken me outside my comfort zone. I'm getting involved in deeper conversations with my clients and the interaction level is way up. I'm experimenting more and getting different outcomes and really learning a lot. There is a lot to keep up with, but overall, the experience has been really positive."

Then he told her about the newsletter he was going to start called "The Ting! Newsletter" She thought it was a good idea and offered her input.

"You know Tony, we talk a lot about critical thinking and people like us in large organizations are very skilled at it. But if you look more deeply, you will find that some of our top analysts are highly intuitive people. Their best insights come from knowing what data to pay attention to and which to ignore.

"Intuitive people often show up as brilliant analysts. I think they are so quick to see a great decision or path to follow and because they also understand cultural dynamics so well, they sense the best way to sell their point of view. In a more open culture, they'd probably be able to do this easier and things could happen faster."

She suggested a couple of senior people that Tony could interview for his newsletter.

"Sounds good," he said. "Those are great suggestions. Are there any other topics you think we should include?"

"Well," Hermilla replied, "yes, there are several. Language and communication are obvious ones that come to mind. One of the things we don't often talk about at work is how much our conversations depend on intuitive elements. That's what happens with text messages. Words aren't the only thing we communicate. There's a lot going on in the subtext of language experience. If someone else read the words and weren't part of the emotional context of the conversation, they probably wouldn't 'get it.' It's complex.

"When we talk, we communicate experience and learning to and from each other. Language and meaning depend on shared experiences. This is a much more intuitive process going on than the words alone would suggest. We convey inner pictures to and from each other, including feelings and meaning associations that contain our intentions, hopes, and desires. That part is very personal. It's more like we are transferring and sharing thoughts and accumulated life experience with each other. This all happens so quickly and intuitively. Successful communication is when these exchanges lead to a personal transformation in one or both of us.

"That's why empaths and people with high empathy levels are such agile communicators. They listen with their inner awareness as much as their ears. Their takeaways from conversations are much higher and people tend to trust them more. In fact, I bet there's a huge correlation with high levels of empathy and high levels of trust."

"That would make total sense," said Tony. "Trust is a currency. People who are more trusted, in a sales role like mine, generate more and higher sales revenues. I'd say high trust also goes along with success in general, whether it's business or personal relationships. I never associated intuition and empathy with trust before, but that feels very right.

"And I agree with what you said about intuition and language. That's fascinating. All this communication and conversation that we participate in, day in, day out, without a second thought. This is amazing when we look at it from a deeper level. I'm definitely going to reflect on this and write something about it. It seems that we need to build a deeper awareness of what's going on during these common processes. And then we need to advocate that to bring out the best in all of us. I'm just amazed at all the latent talent we have, that we aren't even recognizing or appreciating."

"Any others? I'll make a list."

"Yes, we can talk about how to deepen the personal experience of intuition. For example, things like the power of nuance. Nuance is a communicable felt language that translates beliefs and subtle information.

"This fills an emotional gap when feelings don't entirely map into the known or shared experience. It is powerful because listening deeper to what's happening with nuance can lead into the exploration of new unknowns, and seeing new possibilities for change and invention. Nuance is a great way to convey emotional complexity.

"You know that feeling when you have something on the 'tip of your tongue' but can't quite express it or grasp the meaning of something? We need the feeling to recreate the meaning in order to remember it. But meanings have their roots in feeling. So, looking at the entire realm of feeling can lead to really deep insights."

"Absolutely," said Tony. "This would make a great bar conversation. It's intriguing. But where do you see the connection with our work?"

"Ha," said Hermilla. "I knew you were going to ask about that. The basis of all relationships is being able to understand each other and reciprocate – like understanding our customers and clients better, anticipating their needs, finding unfulfilled value, developing new inventions, and innovation. These are outcomes that are very tangible and relevant. It's just that most organizations haven't had a history of connecting the two. But they've always existed. Just like the benefits of meditation existed before academics and scientists proved them.

"The biggest thing on the transformation agenda for businesses and organizations, as the world opens to be more creative, is for them to go deeper. They need to do that so they can grow, adapt, and continue to provide value. For this, transformation is critical."

Tony became silent and did not speak. He was taking it all in. For the first time, many things were making sense and his nervous system was beginning to fuse and synthesize everything. He stayed quiet because that was the only thing he could do. But it was a happy kind of quiet; an inner eureka moment.

Hermilla knew that he had gotten some deep level insight. She remained quiet too. The entire room became quiet and deep and somehow perfect.

Ting! Power #7

Become a Ting! advocate

TING

77

8 THE POWER OF AUTHENTICITY

The mid-morning sun shone brightly in Tony's office. It illuminated two photographs; one, a cliff with a rock-climber ready to scale the peak of a towering rock crest above a canyon, the other, a nature scene of a deep green forest. Both reminded Tony of how much he loved the outdoors.

He'd been on the phone constantly, reworking some of the intermediate project outcomes with his partners. He noticed Jas had come by a couple of times, with an urgency to talk to him about something. This time, Jas came by and poked his head in, catching Tony's eye. They gestured in hand signals to meet in 5 minutes. From the corner of his eye, Tony scanned the last monthly division report.

It looked a little bleak, but he'd been too tied up in the new project to spend much time wondering what the rest of the department was doing.

After completing his call, he hung up and made the roundabout turn down the hall that led to Jas's office. Jas looked up, motioned Tony to sit down, and got up to close the door.

"There have been some developments," Jas said.

Inwardly Tony braced himself. He shuffled his feet under the chair. He'd heard those words before, just as the restructuring was announced five years ago when luckily, he'd been spared the effects of downsizing. Many of his friends hadn't been so lucky.

Jas looked at him directly and continued. "At our last executive meeting, we spoke at length about this new implementation project. The work has been impressive on all sides and the exec's feel there's a lot more to be done. So, with that in mind, they're interested in moving you over to the Research Department and want to create a position for you as a Project Leader. It would be a promotion with a different set of responsibilities and I want to know if you'd be interested."

Tony was unprepared; the impact of the news was so sudden. "Sure," he answered. "Of course, I'm interested."

"I thought you would be. Let me tell you a bit more about the job. It's a new position. You'd be acting as an adjunct between the Sales Division and the Research Division. The purpose of the position is to scope potential new product and service projects and do early development and testing before it moves further into the development channel."

"I'd enjoy that. Sounds like an interesting challenge." Tony replied.

Jas continued: "The first project you'll be working on is the one you're doing now, but as the design for a new product and service offering. The revenues for your project and its value for our client have turned out to be substantial. Several of the executives have been looking at the project as a new business growth area. The marketing group put some stats together and began doing research on the potential need for this among our other clients and the marketplace. Seems that 24% of our existing clients would be interested, and beyond this, 36% of new client prospects would be interested. They want you to take the lead in implementing it."

"That's great," said Tony. "So it's basically to lead a new innovation product."

"Absolutely," said Jas. "In our market, there is

nothing more important right now. In fact, we predict that if we want to grow or even to be consistent, more than a third of our revenues in the next 3 years will have to come from new product and service innovations. That means we have to create and develop them and lead them. We need to become more adept at innovating."

Jas went on. "The great thing is that the majority of executives are on board with it. Even the chairman agrees. So, we have strong support. And they've made a concerted decision that, despite revenue declines, they won't reduce staff. We've invested a lot in our people and we need to take care of them while we transform the company. So they plan to reposition departments along the way and then hire into the knowledge gaps that are created."

"All this came out of a Ting I had? I'm just glad you gave me the initial support to follow through. That was so important!"

"True, we are all fortunate that things happened the way they did. When you think of the probability of this occurring in our normal scope of business, it would have been a moon shot for us. Normally we've got enough to do just keeping up with change.

"Because we run lean, we don't tend to look beyond that. But the time has come for us to transform the way we do business. Cutting costs isn't really the right way to do it. We should be investing more instead. To transform at a level of scale, we've got to change the texture of our thinking to enable more creative and intuitive approaches. We can't afford to leave out this kind of input anymore. It's too risky. This is precisely the opposite of what most people think. They think it's risky to include these approaches.

"Innovation is the out breath of creative solutions to problems. Most organizations haven't learned to draw an in-breath.

"They are masters of execution but not implicit appreciation, in other words, problem absorption, which is what you did with your client. You took the time to really understand what they were struggling with."

"Very true," answered Tony. "I couldn't agree more. If I didn't see it firsthand, I'd probably still be limited that way as well."

"The proof is in the pudding, isn't it? But we'll also have to deliver more to our employees and clients. So, we'll also be looking at ways to measure up to the worthiness of getting their increased commitment and trust. We have to become a company that inspires and delivers the right solutions. That's a two-way process."

"Yes, we have to show how we're making a difference as measured in everyone's eyes; not just our own," replied Tony.

"So…I'll give them an affirmative on your acceptance of the position. They're looking for a start date in four to six weeks. Is that all right?"

Tony nodded.

"Oh, and Tony," Jas asked, "how is the Ting! newsletter going?"

"It's going well. I've interviewed some of the leaders from other divisions at Hermilla's suggestion. They have some amazing stories that I've never heard before. It'll be interesting to see how people respond."

"Yes," said Jas. "It will be."

"Just talking about intuition seems to help people be more authentic," said Tony.

"Of course. When our leaders talk openly about something like this, they are advocating for authenticity and partnership."

Tony thought for a moment and then said "This is so different from our usual expectations of people, which seem to be contrived. You know what I mean,

Jas; the game face you put on to go to work and be what the company needs you to be and hide the rest."

"I know what you mean Tony," Jas said with deep knowing eyes. "But personally, I stopped doing that years ago because I found myself just feeling stressed from it. I think everyone's been conditioned to accept a suppression attitude in employment.

It starts when we're young. We are taught to please teachers, work for grades and recognition. Education is changing somewhat, but it's still stuck there. Then you choose a career direction that suits what people around you value and the opportunities you're offered, which may not be the right ones for you. There's very little thought for other possibilities and other ways to be. But now that's all opening up."

"I have often felt enslaved to the system Jas. And it gets me down sometimes."

"That too, Tony. That's in your head, in your beliefs."

"But it's also true, Jas. Hasn't there always been a system where people struggled for power and those in power tried to subvert others to their will, and where those in power were always the benefactors in the end?"

"I'm not saying that is not also true Tony," Jas said with a smile. "You don't know how many times I've sat in this chair talking to people who were at the breaking edge. It doesn't matter their race or cultural background, their status, single moms and dads, married people struggling with conflicting directions, I've seen it all."

"Mostly I've seen the damage it does, to them and to myself. The more people subvert themselves to this external authority or try to conform to what they feel is a pressure to commoditize themselves or do more for less, the harder it is for them to continue. The inner stress builds and builds as they try harder and harder to overcome this conflict. There is literally no end but out."

Tony said. "Most people in the country are living this way. They work and work and are burning themselves out. I was almost there a few months ago until I started working with Hermilla, and now you. You've helped me change my perspective."

"Well, that's what I mean," said Jas. "The change has to come from inside. No one outside yourself can free you, not from your circumstances, nor from your beliefs. And the more you hold on to these beliefs, the more you struggle.

"You see, beliefs are much more powerful than

thoughts. They're like thoughts magnified millions of times because they're loaded with emotions, expectations and visions. Often these visions are negative because they represent the face of fear. In this case, the vision is really about the fear of continued enslavement. This is the exact opposite of a vision of freedom.

"By continuing with it, you feed the destructive belief. Do you realize how hard it is to invest all the energy to get over this belief when everything you do is perpetuating it, every single day, in your thoughts, your experiences, the things you say to yourself, the way you interpret conditions around you, assess opportunities, or even miss out?"

"I guess it's quite a lot." said Tony. "When you put it that way, it's no wonder that people end up getting burnt out."

"Yes, burn out is the end of the road. There is really no other outcome, other than built up resentment and pent up anguish that can get released in other terribly destructive ways."

"So again we come back to this - for change to happen it has to come from within. That gets the energy of choice moving again. So long as we believe, what we conceive will reinforce it. We have to go right to that core belief and destroy it or change it."

"That's hard when it has become an entrenched habit," said Tony.

"It can be easy; it can be difficult. Depends on the individual. Sometimes it's just as easy to give up. And by giving up I mean surrendering. Then things like intuition move back into our awareness and start giving us hints and clues about other possibilities. When we begin listening, this opens the door to a new vision and new experiences."

"You know what the hardest question for me is, Jas? What do I really want?"

"Yes," said Jas. "I know what you mean. This IS the hardest question. And that is the precise challenge that freedom poses. Who are you? What do you want?"

"We can't answer any of that from our conditioning or even our past experiences, even though some of the answers may come from that position. There is only one real place to answer this – in our hearts. Some people need to just feel that for a while, to reacquaint themselves. Our society has been so intellectually conditioned and ego-justified. This innocent place is the only place we can go for the deep personal answers we need most."

"The hardest thing, after years of work habits, is to

listen to one's true heart. So first we start to listen and then a Ting will come. And then another, and so on."

"Ultimately," said Tony "I guess we confront our own authenticity."

"Yes, that is what moves the beam." said Jas. "And ultimately, what makes you shine. Truth is not a blueprint. It is the language of authenticity. When everyone is authentic, we all win."

"Wow," said Tony. "This is really powerful. All this has been happening with me but I didn't know how to express it. I was concerned about how far down the rabbit hole we were going to go. And inevitably, that it would stop somewhere because it was incongruent with what we do. But you described it so well. I realize it's not incongruent with anything."

"Absolutely, Tony. None of us know beyond this day how long we will be here, how long we will work here. It used to be that a career was the desired way to pursue your economic growth, status and set a foundation for your life.

"Now it's all about living a life that is worthy of your aspirations. Career may be a part of it, a temporary part of it, or not at all.

"If you are driven as an entrepreneur, what you create becomes your career. Your next project becomes your platform for learning and experimentation.

"No doubt, some of us will make lifelong friends here that we will take with us on our journeys. Others we'll leave behind as our paths continue forward. That's life. If and when it is time for you to go, or for me to, you and I will get that Ting that it is time, that it is right. And everything is ok with the universe."

"Jas, for the first time ever, I feel like the stress I've been carrying for years has been lifted in this conversation. I feel like it has suddenly melted away."

"I am happy Tony that you feel this way. I experienced this too. It opened up a whole new beginning for me."

"So yes, when an organization opens to intuition – it encourages people to be authentic. Organizations spend too much energy married to their thoughts but divorced from their feelings.

"Let's talk more about the newsletter in the coming weeks and see what we might be able to do with this topic," smiled Jas.

He added, "On a personal level, I'm really proud of what you did, conceiving of this newsletter, and going forward with it, even though you were taking a personal risk."

"Yes, now I realize I was taking a personal risk to continue not being enslaved. It doesn't sound much like a risk to me now," Tony laughed. "Thanks, Jas, I appreciate your trust and support."

They shook hands and gave each other a look that said they understood each other completely.

Ting! Power #8

Be willing to excavate your thoughts & beliefs

9 THE HEART OF POWER

It was just before noon on a sunny Wednesday. Tony finished reading the first draft of the newsletter. He decided to drop by Jas's office to see if he could get some feedback on it before it was released.

The door to his office was open so Tony knocked lightly on the door. "Hey Jas, got a few minutes?"

Jas looked up. "Hi Tony. Sure. Come in. I'm just reviewing some potential lease prospects."

"Why?" Tony asked. "Are we moving?"

"Quite likely," Jas answered.

"Is the company trying to save money?" He knew from the smile on Jas' face the answer was no.

"Our lease is up in 18 months. And we're thinking the south part of town is offering a lot of possibilities. New companies are moving in and there's a lot of development happening. It's a chance for us to relocate to where the action is and make some new friends. And new clients!

"It's more expensive but there are lots of great amenities our existing building doesn't have. And it's in a neighborhood with trendy bars, cafés and local music. We're even thinking of building a gym and yoga studio for our staff. Here, check it out!" He slid the report across the desk and it made a soft whooshing noise.

"Oh that's cool," said Tony as he began skimming the pages, getting excited.

"Do you know where the most expensive real estate is, Tony?"

"It used to be Manhattan. Now it's Silicon Valley and San Francisco, I think. Or do you mean internationally, like Dubai, Hong Kong or London?"

"Let's look it up," as he began googling lease rates

in the various areas. Tony got up to watch the screen from behind him. "Ok, here it is…" They quickly reviewed comparables.

"Ok, so we know what the rates are and ours looks like a pretty sweet deal. But that's not the most expensive real estate. Do you know what is?"

Tony nodded, "Nope…I guess I don't then."

Jas flashed him an 'I got you again' smile and said: "It's that quarter of a square foot between your ears." He began laughing. So did Tony, as he got the point.

Let's see what that's worth. He began googling it and soon found the answer he wanted. "Advertisers spend around $1 trillion annually for that quarter square foot of space. So that would be over $8 trillion per square foot."

"That is a lot," said Tony. "But I'm betting there's an even smaller space they should be aiming for – the heart."

"That is true Tony. But the sad fact is, the war between the head and the heart has already been won. Most people live in their thoughts so that's still a point of maximum return for marketers. But the thought world is a very noisy and competitive one. As that gets redirected, and this IS happening, it will change a lot of things."

"I agree Jas," said Tony.

Jas smiled. "The energy of 100 or a 1,000 people who care a little is no match for the energy of a 100 or a 1,000 people who care a lot.

"So you wanted to see me about something else, I imagine."

Tony smiled, "Yes, I was hoping you'd want an early read on the Newsletter draft. Here it is. If there's anything you think should be added or changed, now's the time to tell me."

They reviewed it together for a few minutes with Jas recommending a few minor changes.

"Great. Thanks so much," said Tony. "It's off to distribution now."

Ting! Power #9

Let your heart speak louder than your mind

10 GOING DEEPER

Hermilla stared blankly out the window. It had been a long day. She was up late the night before because one of her children had gotten sick during the night. She was tired.

She wanted to leave but remained planted in her chair, her legs resting on a stack of file boxes. She was daydreaming about times long past when she and her husband used to be able to plan things spontaneously and spend the day going places, just the two of them. She missed that and knew he did too. They'd have to find a way to get some time out together soon. She called him and asked how their daughter was doing. They talked for a bit. Upon hearing a good report, she decided she would linger a bit longer.

Tony didn't know why he decided to pass through Hermilla's floor. But he did. Thinking she had left for the day, he was surprised to pass her office and find her there. He stopped and asked how she was.

"Hi Tony," she said, "It's good to see you." Then she explained why she hadn't left.

Tony listened intently. "I can't imagine what it's like to have to plan to have time together. But then I don't have children yet, so I expect that will change once we do."

Tony wanted to say something about his meeting with Jas yesterday. So he explained their discussion to Hermilla adding, "Something is still bugging me deep down. Are we all somehow doomed by this work-work lifestyle? I mean, look at you. You're tired, you've put in a full day here, you want to go home and you don't even have the energy to leave. I know you need to catch a train to get there. You won't be home for another hour or so, even if you leave now."

"That's true," said Hermilla. "But it gets quiet around here at this time and I kind of like it. I'm not working anymore. It gives me time to reflect and get some space, even if I am tired. I wouldn't get that at home until late at night, and by then I'd probably just fall asleep."

"So, this is a personal oasis for you."

"Yes," said Hermilla, "very much so.

"So, Tony, what is it that's bothering you about the conversation you had with Jas?"

"Well, I keep thinking about the experience of being inside an organization; the internal politics and things like that. I know it shuts people down. Some people take their roles so seriously. It's hard to have a real conversation with them outside of that. Do you know what I mean?"

Hermilla nodded. "Yes, I do, Tony. I've seen it a lot. These are mostly the pleasers. They do what they think they have to do, not what they feel they have to do. They're often inauthentic as a result."

"Exactly," said Tony. "I mean if other people are here because they like what they do, they still have to deal with people who don't have the same motivation. So, I wonder if organizations can really change and be places where power can be brokered more openly. I realize we can't make people change unless they want to."

Hermilla looked Tony directly in the eye and said: "If you are authentic, that's all that's needed for change to begin."

"Oh, come on, Hermilla. I don't think we can just extricate ourselves from all that. We have to look after ourselves because those others can hurt us or interfere with our own progress."

"Oh, so you're advocating to be more self-interested in your own defense, than in your authenticity? You can't be both. Either you are authentic, or you aren't."

"Ughhh" said Tony. "I knew you'd say that. You're relentless." He clutched his hand to his heart dramatically.

"And you are the rubber chicken on the ice. The game is already over. The bird is dead and fried."

Tony looked taken aback. A moment of awkward silence followed.

Then she spoke "Yes, Tony, this is a very particular quandary. It's not just your quandary. Every person struggles at some level with this issue. It starts as soon as we realize that our power isn't enough. We start to deploy tactics to get what we want. Then we begin to tamper with energy, our own, and that of others to try and get something from them. That's where the self-subterfuge begins, and we start to erode our intuition and become inauthentic. It's the core dilemma of self and society.

"It's often a dirty game," said Hermilla. "We all play it.

"But this game has been going on for ages - from the first day a person realized he or she could deviate from their authenticity to engage in a struggle for power. That is what broke the cycle of authentic energy. And since then, institutions of all kinds have been trying to do the same, to take over from the split. I don't care what kinds of institutions, whether they are religions, educational institutions, corporations, social groups, governments… They all do this."

Tony stopped reacting to his argument and began listening intently. This was something important he felt.

"Well", he said, "what if it stopped?"

"We'd be living in a different kind of world, a different kind of society and a lot of things would change simultaneously."

Hermilla continued, "The core truth here is that your intuition has primacy. It's the first relationship you have with your body. Intuition is the deep intelligence of all things, conveyed to you as an individual self –a direct and perennial connection with your being. It is pure life principle, soul, core energy, whatever you want to call it. Deep cognition. Everything else comes after that. Even beliefs. It's an innocent relationship. Uncoloured. Unconditioned. This is the real meaning of authenticity and staying true to yourself. It is self-sovereignty. Your own creative autonomy.

"Certain groups long ago found ways to exploit that to control others and influence their beliefs and condition them around beliefs that would be advantageous to those who wanted to hold power.

"Our relationship with that power, authentic power, is bigger than we know. Even if we describe the universe as a living moving dish of quantum spaghetti, that power knows where to go immediately and get what you want or need, whether or not you know what that is.

"You direct the flow from any point. When you deprive yourself, because other kinds of conditioning got in there and reshaped you, it can be a struggle to find it again. But still, it remains easy and accessible. It happens through intuition.

"So, what happens when you connect with it? You stay authentic. You go where you need to go. You become who you need to become. The right people come to you.

"More than a job or career, people want a life they can be truly present in. The you that you can become has nothing to do with your job or who you think you are.

"When you're authentic you don't need to worry about the impact others have. Your personal power becomes a better conduit for energy. Your world and opportunities are not constrained by theirs. It's a better way to live, both within and outside organizations.

"This is the start of a massive energy transformation. Organizations that are brave enough to recognize the primacy of intuition and respect that relationship, stand to gain unprecedented levels of loyalty and commitment from their leaders, staff, and customers. That helps people tap into their core creative energy and what they want to accomplish as an individual while they are helping their organization achieve its goals. And that is what will inspire true partnership, even companionship, to support."

Tony felt the truth and energy in her words. But he was not there. He was in memories of long ago, his mind drifting to times when he'd sought that same authenticity.

Hermilla tilted her head and looked up as a sudden Ting! landed in her awareness.

She spoke. "The trajectory of authenticity has intuition as its wings."

Hermilla paused there and got up to get her coat. "I should be heading out now." she said to Tony.

Tony got up too. He was still deep in thought as he said goodbye and walked to his car.

Ting! Power #10

Reset your inner default so intuition is first

11 SHARING TING!

The Ting! Newsletter

Welcome to the Ting! Newsletter. You're probably wondering why we picked this name for it. We're hoping it would make you curious to find out what a Ting! is.

Ting! is a made-up word for what happens when we get struck by an intuition or insight, hunch, gut feeling, or some other perceptual event. A Ting! is that first inner cue that prompts us to pay attention.

We think Ting!'s are important. They tell us about things that may not be on our radar. They open our minds to see what's going on at a deeper level. They're important for creativity and innovation too.

Ting!'s can help to make our company and the world a better place. So, we're encouraging you to share your Ting!'s and help us create a welcoming environment and open innovation culture where they can flourish and you feel encouraged to communicate them. That way, we all benefit personally, professionally and organizationally.

The goal of this newsletter is to:

1. Share insights
2. Provoke thought and dialogue
3. Tell some Ting! stories
4. Learn together
5. See where it leads us

So here are a few stories that you've probably never heard around the water cooler, some from our executives and some from you, the people who make this company great.

Here's how you can help. Talk about it. Ask questions. Send us stories about what you did with an intuition at work and how it helped you or what you learned from it. And please email our editorial team to tell us what kind of learning initiatives or events you'd like to see.

We hope you see this newsletter as the start of something great.

Sincerely yours,

Tony Bonstella
Editor
ting@intuita.com

"Hey, Hermilla!" Tony greeted Hermilla with an enthusiastic smile as he poked his head into her office. "Did you read it yet?"

Hermilla smiled through her raised coffee cup. "The Ting! Newsletter? Yes," she said. "I did. And I loved it! What kind of a reaction have you been getting?"

"Oh, it's been interesting. I had a few people calling me to ask if it was for real. Others, both men and women, called to thank me for doing something like this here and wanted to know how they could participate and contribute.

"Others were chuckling about it in the staff room, but more out of amusement than anything else. What's important is that it's circulating, and people are talking about it. They don't know what to make of it yet but the ice is definitely thawing."

Hermilla nodded affirmingly. "That sounds like a great start!"

Tony said… "Yes, I really didn't know what to expect. It was a risk, just like anything new in a big organization like ours. You have to do something to actually see how people react. But from the sounds of it, people are talking about it in meetings too."

Hermilla reflected for a moment, then said. "It would be great to give people some starters on how to use it at meetings, some examples maybe. Let's see if we can come up with some ideas.

"Actually, did you know that intuitive abilities get magnified in teams?"

"Really?" said Tony, "Wow, that would be a great topic to explore. Let's work on it this week. When are you available?"

"I can do tomorrow morning at 11:30," said Hermilla.

"Good, I'm free then too," said Tony.

"By the way Hermilla, there is one question that keeps coming up for me and I've heard it from others too. Do you have five minutes to talk about it?"

"Sure."

"The question is this: How do I know if it's really my intuition? What if it's wrong?"

"That's a fantastic question Tony and one I've worked on for myself.

"Intuitive clarity or intuitive acuity is something that evolves. First, we learn to recognize it when it happens. Then we learn to trust it until we can distinguish what's really intuition from what isn't. This is a highly individual process that takes practice and commitment to master."

"I think I know what you mean Hermilla," replied Tony. "In the beginning, I wasn't sure if it was really intuition, but as I began to 'go with it,' it got clearer and clearer. Like the episode with my mom that turned out to be so epically real. After that, I was able to relax more and just follow it. I can't explain it well, but for me, there's an inner sense that says 'Pay attention to this.' And I'm more attuned to noticing it now."

"There are two things that are commonly misconstrued as intuition." continued Hermilla. "One is wishful thinking. The other is implicit cognition, in other words, our subjective biases, which typically filter out ideas that don't fit."

Wishful thinking is when someone hopes so much for a certain outcome it skews their perception until it fits with that wish. This is an immature reflex because, when one is truly self-aware, it is possible to notice these things.

So wishful thinking is an ungrounded hope or wish that doesn't align with certainty. This can be sensed. The feeling of solidity is usually missing. People who get misled like this are often doubters who have done nothing purposeful to change the outcome but wish for someone else, or some external condition, to take responsibility for doing that. Because they are not honest with themselves, they misconstrue the result and ignore facts that would back up the truth, in favor of their subconscious bias."

"I can relate to that explanation," said Tony. "How do you reconcile this?"

"I guess the easiest thing is to be honest with yourself and notice the bias. Then sense if the other signal is really a signal, or just the bias asserting itself loudly enough to get attention. Most times, it's the bias showing up, and not intuition at all – which is a prelude to fantasy."

"Hmm… that's good." agreed Tony. "This would be a good topic for the next Newsletter."

"Yes, you should do something on that. And you should mention that self-awareness practices like mindfulness and meditation really help."

Hermilla continued, "Ok, so the second thing, implicit cognition, is the vast system of inner thought and social filters we each have. Each time we communicate or make a decision we process our experiences through these filters. Because it's embedded, implicit, and happens very quickly, the outcomes seem to be intuitive. But they are really opinions filtered through our own subjective thoughts, beliefs, and experiences.

"The range of intuitive experience extends beyond these biases. For example, you may have a strong experience bias to follow a particular route, but suddenly intuition will tell you to go a different way because this time something has changed."

"That sounds a bit like instinct," said Tony.

"You're right. It does behave like instinct. But instinct is a different thing entirely. Instinct is an inherited set of subconscious bias that probably comes from ancestral memories and collective human experience. You know, the kind that warned us about dangerous predators and things like that in our environment. Instinct is responsible for our immediate poise to alertness and motion when we see sudden moving objects. This originates from our older more primitive brain.

"The other kind of subconscious bias comes from the conditioning and choices we made ourselves in our life experience."

"I definitely agree with that," Tony replied.

"Academics and scientists often use the word intuition to mean exactly the kind of implicit cognition we are talking about. When they say something is intuitive they mean the solution doesn't conflict with their experience, assumptions, beliefs and known theories. This is really filtration, not intuition."

"That's funny," said Tony, "yes, I can see that. True intuition would present them with an exception scenario or different variables."

"Yes, said Hermilla, "But real innovators use their intuition to understand the problem better, and because they're better with problem absorption, they develop better solutions.

"Many inventions and discoveries end up challenging the status quo, so it might seem that the traditional scientific thought system is biased to present congruence, not intuition, which slows things down. In that system, intuition becomes a problem, which requires objective proof. But that raises the other problem, which is that intuition is completely subjective and often cannot be proven. But it can definitely lead to a prototype for something new, perhaps unrelated in scope to the original problem. And while some people are good at noticing intuition, others aren't.

"We stand to gain a lot more in innovation with the cognitive diversity that intuition brings and the results, speed and action that happen outside the classroom or lab container.

"When we look at problems and solutions from a level of deep cognition, things can look very different. That's where good intuition comes in handy.

"When we don't want change, we have the comfort of our thoughts. When we desire change, we have the comfort of our intuition.

"One thing intuition teaches is that you can't rely on your comprehension. When you become good at listening to your intuition, you have access to a sense apprehension that surpasses everything you think you understand."

"That," said Tony, "is definitely going to be my takeaway for the day. Thank you Hermilla for the thought-provoking responses."

"Glad I could help Tony. See you tomorrow."

Tony glided out the door deep in thought, reflecting on what he'd just learned.

Ting! Power #11

Share your Ting!'s

12 GOING BEYOND

Two weeks later Tony met in Hermilla's office again after having to reschedule their meeting twice in the same week because of busy schedules. She greeted him warmly.

"A little birdie told me you're getting a promotion! Congratulations."

"Thanks," a clearly happy Tony beamed back.

"Jas told me late last week after a meeting while we were chatting about other things. That's great news."

"Hermilla, I can't even put into words how grateful I am to you for working with me this way. Your teaching and mentoring brought out so much potential I never realized I had."

"I can see that Tony. It's been exciting for me to see those aspects of you come alive. But you did the inner work and were open to making the changes. You had the attitude of a true learner. So, you have to give yourself a lot of credit."

"Yes, I know. But when I look back to where I was before, the inner shifts have been gigantic. It's like I threw a brick in the window of my life and woke up from my work coma. I'm a totally different person now. I experience my life and work more richly. I'm more curious about things, more involved, more engaged. I get up and look forward to my day, no matter what I'm doing."

Hermilla mused, "If you go deeper, you'll discover an interesting relationship among authenticity, intuition and flow. When you are authentic and intuitive, you enter a flow state. When you're in flow, you create. The deeper you go into your authenticity, the more power you have to create."

Tony said "Yes, I agree. That's true. I'd put it this way:

"Authenticity + intuition = Flow. Flow creates."

"I love that! It's a great way to describe it," said Hermilla.

Suddenly Tony glanced up at the clock. "Uh, oh," he said abruptly. "It's 3:30 already. I've got to leave early today. I have a wedding rehearsal to go to."

"Really?" asked Hermilla, still reading the latest edition of the Ting! Newsletter, "Whose?"

"Mine, actually".

"Well you'd better get going then." She got up and embraced him with a warm hug. "Tony I wish you and Sara all the very best."

Tony returned the embrace and nearly flew down the stairs with the lightest heart in the universe. Inwardly a Ting arrived that told him he'd made the right decision. He couldn't wait to see what life had in store for him next.

Ting! Power #12

Trust the process

The 12 Powers of Ting!

1. Say "YES!" to your intuition
2. Do nothing for 5 minutes every day
3. Practice awareness for 10 minutes every day
4. Listen to your intuition. Notice your Ting!'s
5. Pay attention to Ting!'s. Look deeper
6. Connect the dots. Look for opportunities
7. Become a Ting advocate
8. Be willing to excavate your thoughts & beliefs
9. Let your heart speak louder than your mind
10. Reset your inner default. Put intuition first
11. Share your Ting!'s
12. Trust the process

by Arupa Tesolin, Intuita.com

About The Author

Arupa Tesolin is a visionary creative who wonders and occasionally writes about it. She's the founder of Intuita & creator of Intuita MindWare, an intuitive process used to generate breakthrough insights.

Arupa is an international speaker, trainer & consultant in innovation and performance transformation who helps teams and organizations develop a whole innovation mind-set.

She is also the CEO of VELOCIFIED, a talent acceleration company that gets people up to speed faster in any job and an industry expert in learning and development with numerous publications.

Social Media
Linked In: linkedin.com/in/arupatesolin/
Twitter: @arupatesolin
Facebook: facebook.com/arupatesolin
Instagram: @arupatesolin

Contact the Author
intuita.com: Inner skills to create, innovate & transform

VELOCIFIED.com: Enterprise Performance & Talent Acceleration

intuita.com
insight that transforms

SPEAKING TOPICS

Arupa is available to speak at your event or conference on the topic of Intuitive Agility, Insight, Creating and Mindful Innovation.

PRODUCTS & ON-LINE COURSES

Intuita MindWare: Insight generation and breakthrough

Easy Meditation – the last meditation training you will ever need

CORPORATE TRAINING
12 Powers of Ting! Webinar
Intuitive Agility for Leaders
Unleash Your Intuition Skills Workshop
Intuita MindWare – insight breakthrough process
Spark – the Creating Workshop

Corporate orders of Ting! available. Pls contact us.

A SPECIAL TING! BONUS FOR YOU

Sign up at Intuita.com for FREE

THE 5-DAY
INSIGHT TRANSFORMATION

- Develop insight abilities to transform your life, work & business
- Learn valuable intuitive exercises that deepen your self-awareness & provide daily insight

PS. There is a secret buried in Ting! Learn what it is when you sign up

PSS. Did you have an "Aha!" moment or interesting story that happened when you read Ting!?

What is your favorite Ting! quote?

Share it with me at ting@intuita.com and on Facebook

www.ingramcontent.com/pod-product-compliance
Lightning Source LLC
Chambersburg PA
CBHW070501100426
42743CB00010B/1717